日本の美しい かき氷

Japan's beautiful Kakigoori
Ryusuke Koike

小池隆介

旭屋出版

目次

はじめに	04
茶屋花冠本店	06
松月氷室	14
御菓子所 ちもと	24
目白 志むら	30
茶の西田園	42
ティーハウスマユール 宮崎台店	52
浅草浪花家	64
たい焼きなみへい	74
三日月氷菓店	84
セバスチャン	92
和 kitchen かんな	100
雪うさぎ	104
慈げん	108
クラフトカフェ	116
あずきや安堂	126
梅むら	132
氷削機・池永鉄工株式会社	138
氷削機・中部コーポレーション	142
明治時代の業務用氷削機	146
昭和のおうちかき氷機	147
あとがき	150

Contents

In the beginning	04
Chaya Hanakanmuri Honten	06
Shogetsu Himuro	14
Okashidokoro Chimoto	24
Mejiro Shimura	30
Cha No Nishidaen	42
Tea House Mayor Miyazakidai	52
Asakusa Naniwaya	64
Taiyaki Namihei	74
Mikazuki Hyokaten	84
Sebastian	92
Wa Kitchen Kanna	100
Yukiusagi	104
Jigen	108
Craft Cafe'	116
Azukiya Ando	126
Umemura	132
Ikenaga Iron Works Co., Ltd	138
Chubu Corporation-Network	142
Ice-shavingg machines in the Meiji era	146
History of household ice-shaving machines	147
Epilogue	150

はじめに

　四季がある日本では、その季節にだけ食べるお菓子があります。

　寒い冬にはぜんざいやおしるこ、春には桜餅や柏餅、蒸し暑い夏はかき氷、秋は栗きんとん。

　他の季節に食べないというわけではないのですが、日本の気候の変化に伴って、どの和菓子屋でも一斉にメニューを変えてゆくのです。

　かき氷は、西暦1000年ごろにはすでに食べられていたという記述が残っており、現在まで食べ継がれてきた非常に歴史の長い日本の伝統食です。

　しかし夏の短い季節にしか提供されないため専門店が少なく、かき氷を伝える文書なども多くありません。

　かき氷とはとても儚い食べ物です。出来上がってから食べ頃はわずか数分。

　どんなに美しい盛り付けをされていても、じっくり眺めている時間はありません。

　かき氷は美しい姿をしている瞬間が、一番美味しい瞬間なのです。

「美しく盛り付けても適当に盛り付けても、口に入れば味は同じ」という人はいるかもしれませんが、

　日本人は「五感で味わう」ということをとても大切にしてきました。

　感触（冷たさ）・味・香りの他に、耳（名前）と眼（美しさ）を含めて食べ物を楽しむのです。

　その一瞬の美味しさ・美しさを一枚の写真の中に閉じ込めました。

Prologue

In Japan, we eat certain sweets during certain seasons.

Zenzai and oshiruko (azuki bean soup) in the cold winter, sakura-mochi (rice cake wrapped in salt pickled cherry blossom leaves) and kashiwa-mochi (rice cake wrapped in oak leaves) in the spring, kakigori (shaved ice with flavored syrup) in the sweltering summer and kuri-kinton (boiled and mashed sweetened chestnuts) during the fall.

These sweets can be eaten throughout the year, but usually wagashi (traditional Japanese confectionery) shops alter their menu according to the changing seasons.

It is said that kakigori can be dated back as far as the year 1000. It is a traditional Japanese dessert which has been passed down through generations. However, because kakigori is only served during the short summer season, shops and artisans that specialize in kakigori are rare.

This fleeting dessert must be eaten quickly after it is served. We do not have time to admire how beautiful it is before it starts to melt. The delicious taste of kakigori peaks when it is visually most beautiful.

Some may say "it all tastes the same no matter how beautifully it is presented", but Japanese people have always valued enjoying food through the senses.
We savor our foods through feeling (coldness), taste, scent, hearing (names) and eyesight (beauty).

In this book, we have captured the transient moment of beauty and lusciousness of kakigori into one picture.

けずりひ

日本最古のかき氷「けずりひ」について

　初めてかき氷が日本の文献に現れたのは平安時代のこと。

　平安時代といえば夏でも着物を着込んだ貴族たちが古書に描かれており、エアコンも電化製品もなかった時代にこのような姿で過ごせると言うことは、現在の夏事情よりも涼しい状態だったのだろうかと想像されるのが自然だが、実は平安時代の夏は平均37度から38度もあったという記述が残されていることから、とても過ごしにくくかつ過酷であったと言うことがわかる。

　暑さをしのぐ手段として取り入れられたのが天然氷であり、冬の間に寒冷地で出来た氷を夏まで氷室で保存しておき、氷柱を立ててうちわで扇いで冷風を送ったり、甘酒を冷やしたりなど、冷蔵用として使用されていた記述が残っている。

　かき氷に関して描かれている最古の記述は、女流作家・清少納言の「枕草子」の中にある。

「削り氷にあまづら(甘葛)入れて，あたらしき金鋺（かなまり）に入れたる」
(清少納言)

　好奇心旺盛であると思われる清少納言は、小さくなった氷柱のかけらを口の中に放り込んでみたのであろうか。冷たい氷を食べることで体温が下がり、爽快感が得られることに気づいたに違いない。

　天然氷を細かく削り、植物から抽出した甘味料をかけてかき氷を食べる様子を「あてなるもの＝上品なもの」として描き残したのだ。

　清少納言の枕草子が完成したと思われるのは長保3年（西暦1001年）。今から1000年を超える夏の暑い日に、かき氷の歴史は京都で始まったと思われる。

　あまづら（甘葛）に関しては正式なレシピは残されていなかったが、日本食文化研究に明るい「茶屋花冠本店」主人の松本栄文氏によって美しい琥珀色の蜜をかけたかき氷が1000年の時を超えて再現が実現した。

Kezurihi

The oldest kakigori in Japan, "kezurihi"

The first record of kakigori in Japan can be dated back to the Heian period (794 - 1185). Some may assume that summer temperatures were cooler in this period when they see people dressed in kimonos living in homes without air conditioning, but records show that they lived through harsh summers with temperatures of up to 38℃.

People in the Heian period used natural ice to cool down during the sweltering summer. Naturally grown ice was stored in specialized ice houses and was utilized to create cold winds, cool drinks and preserve foods. The oldest book to mention kakigori is "The Pillow Book" (Makura no Soshi) written by Sei Shonagon, a lady of the imperial court.

In this book, kakigori made from thinly shaved natural ice with sweet amazura vine (natural sweetener used in Japan made from local ivy) syrup is described as an "elegant dish" and Sei Shonagon writes about how refreshing and cooling it is to eat the ice.

"The Pillow Book" is said to have been completed in the year 1001. From this, we can assume that the history of kakigori started on a hot summer day in Kyoto more than 1000 years ago.

Although no books had recorded the recipe for this amazura vine syrup, Mr. Matsumoto, the owner of "Chaya Hanakanmuri Honten" and an expert on Japanese food culture, was able to recreate this kakigori with beautiful golden-brown syrup after 1000 years.

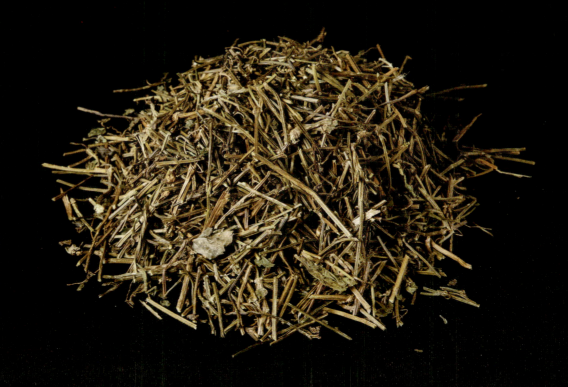

あまちゃづる
Amachazuru (Jiaogulan tea)

「茶屋花冠本店の『あまづらのけずりひ』」 あまづらの削り氷　甘茶蔓（あまちゃづる）
"Amazura no kezurihi" from "Chaya Hanakanmuri Honten" - amachazuru (Jiaogulan tea)

江戸時代の御氷を再現
茶屋花冠本店

　千葉県佐原の伝統建築物保存地区の中心地にある「茶屋花冠本店」では、江戸時代後期の御禁裏（宮中）で流行した宇治金時を提供している。この宇治金時は、日本食文化研究に明るい食品学者の主人松本栄文氏が、徳川将軍家御物茶師として最高位に君臨した京都宇治「三星園上林三入本店」主人上林三入と「古文書」を読み解き再現したものである。

　抹茶のかき氷が誕生したのは、清少納言が「あまづらのけずりひ」を口にしてから約600年後、豊臣秀吉が政権を握っていた時代のことだった。この時代は茶の湯が大変栄えており、秀吉に仕えていたのは有名な茶人・千利休であった。秀吉はかき氷にきび砂糖と抹茶をかけて食べ、これが宇治氷の原点となったと思われる。その後、江戸時代になると甘党で知られる徳川家康が宇治氷に粒あんを添え、現在の宇治金時の形が出来上がったのである。やがてこの宇治金時は御禁裏（宮中）に伝わり、つぶあんより手のかかる「ハレの（特別な）食材」であるこしあんが添えられるようになったのである。

　「茶屋花冠本店」では、当時宮中で食べられていたかき氷を忠実に再現。氷の上にきび糖をふりかけ、昔ながらの製法で作られた抹茶をたっぷりと振る。美しい苔で覆われたような、芸術的なかき氷の上に添えられるのは、時間をかけて練り上げた三度炊きのこしあん。　氷・砂糖・抹茶と餡が口の中で溶け合い、貴族でしか味わえ得なかった極上の味を体験することができる。佐原という歴史情緒あふれる町並みで、日本古来の伝統食・かき氷の味を楽しんでみてはいかがだろう。

　清少納言が食べた「削り氷」と家康や公家衆が食べていたと思われる「宇治金時」は、佐原本店の他、二子玉川の「花冠陽明庵」で提供されている。（二子玉川店は夏季限定・要予約）

Kakigori from the Edo period
Chaya Hanakanmuri Honten

At "Chaya Hanakanmuri Honten", you can enjoy "Uji-kintoki" (kakigori with powdered green tea and sweet azuki beans), which was eaten in the Imperial Palace during the late Edo period. The owner, Mr. Matsumoto is an expert on Japanese food culture. He recreated this Uji-kintoki by analyzing ancient documents and high-quality tea from "Mitsuboshien Kanbayashi Sannyu Honten".

Matcha kakigori appeared 600 years after the first kakigori was mentioned in a book by Sei Shonagon. Japanese tea ceremonies were very popular during this time and it is said that Toyotomi Hideyoshi, a famous warlord, first started eating ice topped with cane sugar and matcha. Later, another famous warlord named Oda Nobunaga topped azuki beans on top of this matcha kakigori and created Uji-kintoki. This kakigori topped with luxurious koshi-an (smooth red bean paste) became a delicacy within the palace.

The taste of this Uji-kintoki has been faithfully recreated at Chaya Hanakanmuri Honten. Cane sugar and plenty of powdered green tea is sprinkled on the ice with slowly cooked koshi-an on top. The flavors of ice, sugar, matcha and azuki beans blend and melt in your mouth. Come visit the historic town of Sawara and enjoy this beautiful and artistic kakigori eaten in the Imperial Palace.

The kezurihi enjoyed by Sei Shonagon and Uji-kintoki enjoyed by Nobunaga can also be enjoyed at "Youmeian Hanakanmuri" in Futakotamagawa (reservation required during the summer season).

「宇治金時の御氷」 きび砂糖・初むかし（御詰め上林三入）・三度炊きのこしあん
"Uji-kintoki no Okori" - cane sugar, Hatsu-mukashi matcha (from "Kanbayashi Sannyu"), koshi-an

茶屋花冠本店

「宇治金時の御氷」
"Uji-kintoki no Okori"

店舗情報
住所：千葉県香取市佐原イ1902-4
TEL：090-4530-0022
かき氷提供期間：通年
かき氷提供時間：10:00~17:00
定休日：月曜
価格帯：1200円

Store information
Address:1902-4 Sawara-i, Katori-shi, Chiba
TEL:+81-90-4530-0022
Kakigori serving period:all year
Kakigori serving time:10:00 – 17:00
Closed:Mondays
Price range:1200 yen

日光の冬を味わうかき氷
松月氷室

　創業明治27年、日光市今市の松月氷室は、古来からの天然氷製法にこだわり続ける、数少ない生粋の天然氷蔵元だ。「天然氷」とは、山間の整氷池に滅菌ろ過した湧き水あるいは地下水を貯め、自然の冷気だけで凍らせた氷のことを指す。上質な天然氷を作るためには、気象、地形、源水などいくつかの条件が揃わねばならず、松月氷室の所有する天然氷池はその全てを満たしているという。

　例えば、氷が作られる1月の夜から朝にかけての温度が−5度前後に保たれる寒さがあり、雪が少ない気象地域であること。氷池の南側が山になっており、高い木々で日光を遮り池全体に直射日光の当たらない環境であること。そのほか数多くの条件を満たす場所は、山の多い日本でもそう多くない。

　松月氷室では、夏が終わると休ませていた氷池の掃除や整地・修復工事を済ませ、天然ろ過装置を手入れするのに約二ヶ月間。気の遠くなるような地道な作業が続く。12月の中頃から氷池に湧き水を引き、あとは冬の冷気で自然に凍るのを待つ。人間はただ見守るしかできないのだ。氷が育っていく間に雨や雪が降れば、せっかく育ってきた氷を割って捨て初めからやり直しだ。切り出しまで後少し、という時に雪が降れば、一晩中徹夜で雪を掃き続けることもある。その姿は「自然との根比べ」のようだ。

　1日中日陰が保たれる風通しの良い場所で、且つ冷たい風の吹き抜ける構造の氷池で、天然氷は1日わずか1cmほどずつ厚みを増す。こうして約2週間の長い時間をかけて14〜15cmの厚さになったらいよいよ切り出しだ。切り出しは「これまでの苦労が一気に報われる収穫の喜びの瞬間だ」と蔵元は語る。

　松月氷室では、この天然氷を使ったかき氷を昔ながらの卸売店舗の店先で販売。自然が育てた氷の味を存分に味わうことができる。

The taste of Nikko's winter
Shogetsu Himuro

Founded in 1894, "Shogetsu Himuro" is a rare ice house still producing natural ice through traditional methods. Natural ice is produced by naturally freezing sterilized and filtered natural water. High quality ice can only be produced under appropriate weather, terrain and water conditions. The ice making pond at Shogetsu Himuro remarkably meets all these conditions.

For example, outside temperature must stay around -5 during the night with little snow and a mountain with tall trees should be located on the southern side of the pond to shade the ice. Even in mountainous Japan, it is very difficult to find an ideal spot.

After the summer, inconspicuous efforts are made to prepare and adjust the ice growing environment. After the pond is filled with water, all we can do is wait for nature to take its course. If snow or rain falls, ice is thrown away and started from scratch. Sometimes staff sweep snow off the ice all night if it snows on ice ready for harvest.

Even in an ideal environment it takes around 2 weeks for the ice to grow to 14-15cm in thickness ready for harvest. The owner says all efforts feel rewarded during harvest.

The taste of naturally grown ice can be enjoyed through varieties of kakigori served at the storefront of Shogetsu Himuro. Come and enjoy kakigori covered in colorful "rainbow" syrup, "Tochiotome strawberry" syrup, or other popular types of kakigori topped with fruits and whipped cream.

天然水の切り出し風景
Harvesting natural ice

氷室（ひむろ）の中は天然氷で埋めつくされる
The himuro (ice house) is filled with natural ice

日光の美味しい天然水がゆっくり凍った、硬く美しい天然氷
Hard and beautiful natural ice created by slowly freezing the tasty natural water of Nikko

「レインボー」シロップ・食紅・香料
"Rainbow" - syrup, food coloring, fragrance

「とちおとめ」 とちおとめ果汁・砂糖
"Tochiotome" - Tochiotome strawberry juice, sugar

「生いちごプレミアム」 苺・砂糖・ホイップクリーム・ヨーグルト・牛乳・練乳
"Fresh strawberry premium" - strawberries, sugar, whipped cream, yoghurt, milk, condensed milk

松月氷室

「レインボー」

店舗情報
住所：栃木県日光市今市379
TEL：0288-21-0162
かき氷提供期間：通年
かき氷提供時間：11:00～18:00（冬期は早じまいあり）
定休日：月曜（祝日の場合は営業、翌火曜休み）
価格帯：400～900円（税別）

Store information
Address:379 Imaichi, Nikko, Tochigi Prefecture
TEL:+81-288-21-0162
Kakigori serving period:all year (at main store)
Kakigori serving time:11:00 - 18:00
　　　　　　　　　　(early-closing during the winter)
Closed:Mondays (if a national holiday, the store will open on Monday and close on Tuesday)
Price range:400 - 900 yen (excluding tax)

和菓子屋のかき氷 1
御菓子所 ちもと

　戦前に東京の道灌山（日暮里）で創業した「ちもと」本店は、その後銀座２丁目に移転。当時は高級料亭で出される手土産や、富裕層のおつかい物として非常に人気があったという。昭和20年代になると、人気の「ちもと」の和菓子を別荘地でも楽しんでもらおうと、軽井沢や箱根などの人気の別荘地に支店を出した。この「軽井沢ちもと」で修行を積み、目黒区八雲に「御菓子所 ちもと」を開店させたのが、現在の店主の先代である。八雲には「軽井沢ちもと」を贔屓にしていた常連客の自宅が多く、また目黒や世田谷に住む文豪・歌手・事業家など多くの人々がこの店の味を愛し、口々にその美味しさを広めてくれたのである。

　「ちもと」がかき氷を提供し始めたのは昭和57年頃。かき氷の中に自慢の和菓子をたっぷり詰めて、茶道に使う美味しいお茶と甘いミルクを半分づつかけたかき氷が大人気になった。やがて夏季限定のかき氷提供期間の間中、店の前はかき氷目当ての行列が絶えなくなった。

　店内はわずか10席。イタリア製の家具が設えられた落ち着いた空間で、外の喧騒から遮断され異空間に入ったような気分になる。運ばれてきたかき氷は、初雪がやさしく積もったような粉雪状で、細かい氷にシロップがしっとりと染み込み、その大きさは子供の頭ほどもあるだろうか。「最初はここまで大きくなかったはずなんだけれど、お客さんの喜ぶ声を聞いているとついつい大きくなってしまう」と店主石原さんは語ってくれた。昔も今も「ちもと」は「ちもと」を愛してくれるお客さんのために、変わらぬ味のお菓子を提供し続けている。お客様に寄り添って歩む姿勢がとても印象的な名店である。

Kakigori from wagashi shops 1
Okashidokoro Chimoto

"Chimoto" was first established before the war at Dokanyama (Nippori) in Tokyo, then later relocated to Ginza 2-chome. At the time, wagashi sold at Chimoto was a popular gift amongst the wealthy and high-class restaurants. From around 1945, Chimoto opened new shops in popular resort towns such as Karuizawa and Hakone. The owner of "Okashidokoro Chimoto" in Yakumo trained at "Karuizawa Chimoto". Many of the regular customers that would visit the resort towns lived around Yakumo and the name quickly spread as literary figures, singers and entrepreneurs spoke about their love for Chimoto.

    Chimoto first started serving kakigori from around 1982. The kakigori was filled with their famous wagashi and topped with sweet milk and high-quality tea. This kakigori became so popular that long lines of people waiting to taste the delicacy was seen almost every day during the summer.

    This shop with only 10 seats is furnished in Italian furniture and the tranquil environment lets us escape from the outside noise. Shaved ice resembling powder snow is softly arranged on the bowl to a heap as large as a child's head with syrup seeping through the fine ice. The owner, Mr. Ishihara says, "it didn't start out this big, but I couldn't help it when I saw how excited the customers were". Chimoto, a prestigious shop that cherishes their customers, will continue to serve sweets for customers who love the taste of Chimoto.

季節とともに変化してゆく和菓子がぎっしり入っている。
スプーンで食べやすいように小さく整えられている。
The bowl is packed with seasonal wagashi,
arranged into small pieces so it is easier to eat with a spoon.

「お任せかき氷」 抹茶蜜・ミルク・八雲餅・白玉・草団子・栗など、季節の和菓子を十数種
"Chef's choice kakigori" - green tea syrup, milk, more than ten types of seasonal wagashi

御菓子所 ちもと

「お任せかき氷」

店舗情報
住所：東京都目黒区八雲1-4-6
TEL：03-3718-4643
かき氷提供期間：梅雨明け〜９月のお彼岸前後
かき氷提供時間：10:00~17:30
定休日：木曜
価格帯：700円〜1100円（税別）

Store information
Address:1-4-6 Yakumo, Meguro-ku, Tokyo
TEL:+81-3-3718-4643
Kakigori serving period:after rainy season to around mid-September
Kakigori serving time:10:00 - 17:30
Closed:Thursdays
Price range:700 - 1100 yen (excluding tax)

和菓子屋のかき氷2
目白 志むら

　昭和14年に青山で開店、その後昭和21年頃に現在の場所に移転した「志むら」は目白で人気の和菓子店だ。開店の翌年から夏季限定で提供されるかき氷が美味しいと評判になり、夏になると2階から1階までの階段を埋め尽くす行列ができるようになった。味だけではなく、かき氷のビジュアルが非常に珍しく、「東京で食べたいかき氷」といえば必ず取り上げられる。断崖絶壁のように反りたったかき氷と、まるで滝のようにかかるイチゴのシロップ。人はそのかき氷を「志むらの崖」と呼ぶ。この個性的なビジュアルはどうして出来上がったのだろうか。

　昭和21年頃、かき氷の提供をはじめた「志むら」では、自家製のあんこなど重めの具材や蜜を氷に乗せる時に、その重さでかき氷が潰れて硬くなってしまうことを懸念していた。試行錯誤の末、ふわりと削ったかき氷は柔らかく積んで崖のように盛り、氷が潰れないように斜面部分にシロップをかけて提供するようになったという。このかき氷を見たお客さんが「まるで崖のようだね」といったことでより意識するようになり、現在のような美しく迫力のあるかき氷ができたという。

　「志むら」のかき氷は、和菓子の世界から生まれたかき氷である。和菓子はたくさんの種類の砂糖を使いこなし、舌触りのよい餡や蜜を作り分ける。その技術はかき氷のレシピの中にふんだんに盛り込まれており、素材に合わせた砂糖の選び方が「志むら」のかき氷の鍵となっているのだ。そして味はもちろん、見た目の美しさ・繊細な形にも細心の注意を払い、一瞬で溶けてしまうかき氷に徹底して美しさを追求している。日本が古来から大切にしてきた、儚いものを愛でる日本の気質が形になったようなかき氷である。

Kakigori from wagashi shops 2
Mejiro Shimura

"Shimura" is a popular wagashi shop first established in Aoyama in 1939 and soon relocated to Mejiro in 1945. Shimura started serving kakigori in 1940 only during the summer season. Their kakigori became so popular that long lines filled their staircases in summer. It has been featured as "the kakigori to eat in Tokyo" many times. The kakigori here takes a unique form. The shaved ice stands like a steep cliff with strawberry syrup running along it like a waterfall. The customers call it "the cliff of Shimura".

When Shimura first started serving kakigori, they were concerned about the ice being crushed by heavy toppings such as home-made anko (red bean paste) and sauce. After many trial and errors, the fluffy ice was arranged in the shape of a cliff and sauce was poured down the slope to prevent the ice from being crushed. The shop became conscious about the shape of the ice after they heard many customers comment on it saying "it looks just like a cliff", resulting in this beautiful and dramatic form.

The kakigori at Shimura comes from the world of wagashi where different types of sugars are used to create various textures pleasant on the tongue. This technique is the key to the delicious taste of Shimura. Considerable amount of care is put into not only the taste, but for the delicate shape of the ice. At Shimura, beauty is pursued in the world of short-lived kakigori expressing Japanese people's age-old love for transient beauty.

「生いちご」 生苺・糖蜜
"Fresh strawberry" - fresh strawberries, sugar syrup

「生いちご」 生苺・糖蜜
"Fresh strawberry" - fresh strawberries, sugar syrup

「白玉」こしあん・糖蜜白玉
"Shiratama" - koshi-an (smooth red bean paste), shiratama (rice-flour dumplings) with sugar syrup

「うぐいす」 うぐいすあん（北海道産青えんどう豆）・うぐいす鹿の子・白玉
"Uguisu" - uguisu-an (green bean paste), uguisu kanoko (sweet green beans), shiratama

志むら・桜のかき氷

　四季のある日本では、古来から「四季の移ろいを愛でる」ということを大切にしてきた。なかでも、桜に対する思い入れは非常に強い。志むらでは、桜を待つ時期から提供され始める「さくら」かき氷は、リアルタイムの桜の花の咲き具合とリンクするようにその見た目の盛り付けが変わってゆくという。

　花を待つ時期に提供する「さくら」は雪山に桜色がほのかに見えるイメージで、かき氷はやや白っぽい。

　やがて花が咲き進むにつれて桜色は濃くなってゆき、器に添えられる桜の花の塩漬けの数も増えていく。

　最後には花が散り、葉っぱの部分が多くなってくるため、かき氷にも緑色の寒梅粉（和菓子の落雁の原料）が多くかかるようになり、わらび餅が添えられる。

　日本の四季の移り変わりを表現した「和菓子」は食べる芸術品と言われている。和菓子屋のかき氷は、眼・感触（冷たさ）・味・香り・耳（名前）で楽しむことのできる素晴らしい氷菓子である。

Shimura / Sakura kakigori

Traditionally, Japanese people have cherished the changing of seasons. Spring time is especially loved as sakura (cherry blossoms) start to bloom. The "sakura kakigori" served at Shimura changes its appearance according to how sakura is blooming outside.

Before the bloom, the slightly white kakigori represents sakura starting to bloom in the snow. The pink color of the kakigori becomes more distinct and more salt pickled flowers are placed on the ice as sakura bloom outside. When the flowers start to fall and green leaves start to sprout, the kakigori is sprinkled with green kanbaiko (glutinous rice flour) and warabi-mochi (bracken-starch dumpling) is placed on the side.

Wagashi is said to be a form of art that represent the changing seasons. Kakigori served at Shimura is a wonderful frozen dessert that can be enjoyed through our senses.

「さくら」 さくらあん・桜の葉の塩漬け・糖蜜・寒梅粉（加熱した餅米の粉）添え蜜（桜白蜜か甘酒蜜）
"Sakura" - sakura-an (cherry blossom flavored bean paste), salt pickled cherry blossom leaves, sugar syrup, kanbaiko (glutinous rice flour), sakura or amazake (sweet fermented rice drink) flavored syrup on the side

「さくら」 さくらあん・桜の葉の塩漬け・糖蜜・寒梅粉（加熱した餅米の粉）添え蜜（桜白蜜か甘酒蜜）
"Sakura" - sakura-an (cherry blossom flavored bean paste), salt pickled cherry blossom leaves, sugar syrup, kanbaiko (glutinous rice flour), sakura or amazake (sweet fermented rice drink) flavored syrup on the side

目白 志むら

店舗情報
住所：東京都豊島区目白3-13-3
TEL：03-3953-3388
かき氷提供期間：通年（11月〜4月は数量限定）
かき氷提供時間：10:00〜18:30LO
定休日：日曜
価格帯：650円〜1500円

Store information
Address:3-13-3 Mejiro, Toshima-ku, Tokyo
TEL:+81-3-3953-3388
Kakigori serving period:all year (limited servings during November to April)
Kakigori serving time:10:00 - last order at 18:30
Closed:Sundays
Price range:650 - 1500 yen

お茶屋さんのかき氷
茶の西田園

　西田園は埼玉県熊谷市妻沼の妻沼聖天山門前町にあるお茶の専門店。創業は明治元年、150年の歴史を持つ風格のある老舗である。創業当時はべっ甲屋として開業したが、やがて日本茶屋へと職を変え、現店主である小林伸光氏でお茶屋としては3代目となる。

　西田園のある埼玉県熊谷市は、国内最高気温を何度も記録したことがあり「日本一暑い街」としても有名な地域でもある。猛暑で知られる熊谷の名物を作ろうと、2006年に「雪くま」というご当地かき氷が誕生した。「雪くま」とは熊谷のおいしい水から作った貫目氷を雪のようにふわふわに削り、各店のオリジナルのシロップを使用した熊谷のかき氷のことで、西田園は2011年に「雪くま」に参加。参加当初からお茶のかき氷で人気を集めていた。2018年には参加店は27店舗となり、「雪くまのれん会」では会長職に就任。今では「雪くま」を引っ張る存在として注目されている。

　かき氷は、お茶を使用したメニューが多く、代表作である「玄米茶あずきみるく」は、試作を重ねて、現在の玄米茶3割・抹茶7割のブレンドに決定。一口含むと、香ばしい玄米茶の風味が口いっぱいに広がり、煎り玄米のカリッとした食感がアクセントになってスプーンが止まらない美味しさだ。
　2018年には本店の正面に「焦がしや武一」というほうじ茶の専門店を開店。自家焙煎機を使って、浅煎り・中煎り・深煎りといった焙煎の調整が自由にできるようになったという。店主曰く、「オリジナルほうじ茶を試行錯誤している」とのことで、ほうじ茶のかき氷の進化も楽しみになってきた。

Tea shops' kakigori
Cha No Nishidaen

"Nishidaen" is a tea shop located in Menuma, Kumagaya City. It was founded in 1868 and is a well-established shop with over 150 years of history. The shop originally specialized in tortoiseshells but transformed into a Japanese tea shop. Mr. Kobayashi, the current owner is the third-generation owner after the shop started specializing in Japanese tea.

Kumagaya is known as the "hottest city in Japan". In 2006, kakigori called "yuki-kuma" was created to promote the city and its tasty water. Currently, 27 shops across town serve their original yuki-kuma. The fluffy ice is topped with original syrup made by each of the shops. Nishidaen started serving yuki-kuma in 2011 and soon became a popular tea flavored kakigori. The owner is now the chairman of the yuki-kuma association.

Japanese tea is used in many of the kakigori served at Nishidaen. It took many tries to create the 3:7 genmaicha (brown rice tea) and matcha blend used for their signature "genmaicha azuki milk (red bean milk)" kakigori. The crunchy roasted rice adds texture to the roasted aroma of genmaicha.
In 2018, the owner opened a new shop specializing in hojicha (roasted green tea) called "Kogashiya Buichi". The shop is now able to make light, medium or deep roast tea with their own roasting machine. The owner says he is now trying to create his own original hojicha, which brings excitement towards a new type of hojicha kakigori in the near future.

「抹茶玄米茶」 玄米を炊いて煎ったものと煎茶をブレンドしたお茶に抹茶を加えたもの
"Matcha genmaicha" - matcha added to a blend of roasted brown rice and sencha (middle-grade green tea)

「玄米茶あずきみるく」 玄米茶・抹茶・ミルクシロップ・炒り玄米
"Genmaicha azuki milk" - genmaicha, matcha, milk syrup, roasted brown rice

「ほうじ茶」 緑茶の茶葉や茎を強火で焙じて製造したお茶
"Hojicha" - tea made by roasting the leaves and stems of green tea

「ほうじ茶あずき」 自家焙煎のほうじ茶を数種類ブレンドしたほうじ茶蜜・あずきかのこ
"Hojicha azuki" - hojicha syrup made from home-roasted hojicha blend, azuki kanoko (sweet azuki beans)

「抹茶」日差しが当たらないように育てた茶葉を粉末状にしたもの
"Matcha" - powdered green tea leaves grown without direct exposure to sunlight

「濃厚抹茶あずきみるく」 静岡産抹茶・あずきかのこ
"Rich matcha azuki milk" - matcha (from Shizuoka), azuki kanoko

茶の西田園

自家焙煎機

店舗情報
住所：埼玉県熊谷市妻沼1523
TEL：048-588-0304
かき氷提供期間：6月～10月（以降は不定期で提供）
かき氷提供時間：11:00~16:00LO（店舗は8:30~19:30）
定休日：月曜・火曜（店舗は火曜営業）
価格帯：600円～900円

Store information
Address:1523 Menuma, Kumagaya-shi, Saitama
TEL:+81-48-588-0304
Kakigori serving period:June - October (occasionally
　　　　　　　　　　　served during off-season)
Kakigori serving time:11:00 - last order at 16:00
　　　　　　　　　　(shop opening hours are 8:30-19:30)
Closed:Mondays (kakigori not served on Tuesdays)
Price range:600 - 900 yen

紅茶を味わうかき氷
ティーハウスマユール宮崎台店

インド紅茶の専門店の「ティーハウスマユール」では、多い時には7～8種類の紅茶のかき氷が揃う。

中でもお薦めなのは　夏季限定で提供される「特製ダージリン」。ダージリンとは紅茶の種類の中で味も香りも最も芳醇であると言われるインドのダージリン地方で採れる茶葉で、年に3回しかない収穫時期の中で香りの豊かなファーストフラッシュ（一番摘み）と味が濃く安定した美味しさのセカンドフラッシュ（夏摘み）をたっぷりと使用。旨味を損なわないようにシロップを抽出する。紅茶好きの人が好むメニューだ。

幅広い層に人気なのは「ミルクティー」や「アッサム＆ディンブラ」のかき氷。ミルクによく合う「アッサムティー」を使用した「ミルクティー」はまるでロイヤルミルクティーのような豊かな味。「アッサム＆ディンブラ」はミルクに合うアッサムと紅茶らしい香りのディンブラをブレンド。そのまま食べてもよし、別添えの紅茶風味の練乳をかけるとミルクティー風に。とてもバランスが良く、紅茶かき氷初心者に試してほしいメニューだ。

冬になると、さっぱりした風味のかき氷より、「マサラチャイ」「ラムチャイ」などのコクのあるかき氷の注文が増える。台湾で流行のタピオカを添えた「タピオカミルクティー」も根強い人気だ。

紅茶のかき氷の他に、お菓子づくりが得意な店主が作る旬の果物の果物蜜も忘れてはいけない。

あまり手の込んだことはせずに、素材の美味しい時に本来の味を生かして仕上げるというのが店主の流儀。四季折々の果物のかき氷が提供されるのを待って、かき氷好きが集まってくる。さくら・あんず・栗・柚子・かぼちゃなど、季節の味がぎゅっと詰まったかき氷を残さず食べ尽くしてみたい。

Black tea flavored kakigori
Tea House Mayoor Miyazakidai

"Tea House Mayoor" is an Indian black tea shop, serving around 7-8 types of black tea flavored kakigori.

The most recommended is the "special Darjeeling" kakigori served only during the summer. Darjeeling tea is said to have the richest aromas out of all black teas. The syrup is carefully extracted from a special blend of first flush and second flush Darjeeling tea.

Appealing to a wider audience is the "milk tea" and "Assam & Dimbula" flavored kakigori. The rich flavor of "milk tea" kakigori is created by Assam tea leaves that match well with milk. "Assam & Dimbula" kakigori is made from a blend of Assam and Dimbula tea leaves full of pleasant aroma. The flavor transforms into rich milk tea when black tea flavored condensed milk is poured on top. I recommend anyone who has never tried tea flavored kakigori to treat yourself to the fantastic balance of flavors.

Rich flavored kakigori such as "masala chai" and "rum chai" is popular in winter and the "bubble tea" kakigori is also very popular. The kakigori inspired by bubble tea popular in Taiwan is served with tapioca balls on the side.

Mayoor is not only about black tea flavored kakigori, but the talented owner makes fantastic fruit syrup made from seasonal fruits.

By using the seasonal fruits at the right timing, the original flavor of the ingredients are emphasized. Kakigori-lovers gather waiting for the seasonal kakigori. I would like to endeavor in tasting all the seasonal flavors including sakura, apricot, chestnut, yuzu and pumpkin.

「ミルクティー」 アッサム紅茶・練乳
"Milk tea" - Assam tea, condensed milk

「マサラチャイ」 紅茶・砂糖・練乳・スパイスシロップ
"Masala chai" - black tea, sugar, condensed milk, spice syrup

「さくらスペシャル」 桜の葉・桜の花・砂糖・桜餡・求肥
"Sakura special" - cherry blossom leaves, cherry blossom flowers, sugar, sakura-an (cherry blossom flavored bean paste), gyuhi (soft mochi)

57

「アボカドミルク」 アボカド・練乳・牛乳・砂糖
"Avocado milk" - avocado, condensed milk, milk, sugar

「柚子ときんかん」 柚子・金柑・砂糖
"Yuzu and kumquat" - yuzu, kumquat, sugar

「いちご」いちご・砂糖・練乳
"Strawberry" - strawberries, sugar, condensed milk

ティーハウスマユール宮崎台店

店舗情報
住所：神奈川県川崎市宮前区宮崎2-3-12-103
TEL：044-854-2430
かき氷提供期間：通年
かき氷提供時間：11:00~16:30LO
　　　　　　　　（土日祝日は11:00~16:00LO）
定休日：不定休（HPやツイッターで要確認）
価格帯：780円~1300円（税別）

Store information
Address:2-3-12-103 Miyazaki, Miyamae-ku, Kawasaki-shi,
　　　　Kanagawa
TEL:+81-44-854-2430
Kakigori serving period:all year
Kakigori serving time:11:00 till last order at 16:30
　　　　　　　　　(last order at 16:00 on weekends)
Closed:irregular holidays (TBA on their website or Twitter)
Price range:780 - 1300 yen (excluding tax)

たい焼き屋のかき氷 1
浅草浪花家

　創業明治42年の老舗「元祖たいやき麻布十番浪花家総本店」で修行を積み、2010年に暖簾分けを許されたたい焼きの専門店「浅草浪花家」。以前店主の祖母が浅草で暮らしていたということから縁を感じたからだという。開店から10年が過ぎ、浅草の街にしっかりと溶け込んできたように見える。

　たい焼きには「天然もの」と「養殖もの」という2種類の焼き方がある。焼きごてのような鋳型で一匹一匹丁寧に焼き上げたものを「天然もの」、一度の6〜10匹以上を焼き上げることができる鉄板タイプの焼き型で大量生産されたものを「養殖もの」と呼ぶそうである。「天然もの」は、一般的に皮は薄皮でしっぽまであんこがたっぷりと詰まっていることが多く、人気が高い。浅草浪花家は総本店と同じ「天然もの」を提供。店先では焼き型を返す音が一日中リズミカルに繰り返されている。

　開店の翌年の2011年、鯛焼きの売上が落ちる夏の間に提供を始めたかき氷が人気となり、今ではかき氷も一年を通して提供。行列が絶えない人気店である。人気の理由は丁寧に薄く削られる口溶けの良い氷と、老舗仕込みの自慢の小豆。巨大な銅鍋で8時間かけて煮られる小豆はつやつやと美しく、豆の香りが非常に豊かで味わい深い。その絶品の小豆に生苺シシロップをかけたかき氷「あさやけ」は、ほっくり甘い小豆に酸味のある生苺という組み合わせが注目を集め、今では浅草浪花家を代表するかき氷となった。

　浅草浪花家のかき氷メニューは常時10〜15種類。春の桜・秋のかぼちゃやおいもなど、四季折々のかき氷を楽しみにしているファンが多くリピーター率が非常に高い。老舗で培われた長年愛される味が、かき氷にも反映されているのであろう。浅草に行けば、その美味しいかき氷にきっと出会うことができる。

Kakigori from Taiyaki shops 1
Asakusa Naniwaya

The owner who trained at "Ganso Taiyaki Azabujuban Naniwaya Sohonten" a taiyaki (fished-shaped cake filled with red bean paste) shop established in 1909 opened his own branch in 2010 called "Asakusa Naniwaya". After 10 years in Asakusa, it seems that the shop has settled in with the traditional atmosphere of the town.

Taiyaki can be made in two ways. "Farm-raised" taiyaki is made in a mold which can bake 6 to 10 taiyaki at a time. "Wild" taiyaki is baked one by one using a special iron tool. The cake-like skin on the "wild" taiyaki is thinner and the red bean paste is filled to the edges. Asakusa Naniwaya serves the same type of "wild" taiyaki as the main shop in Azabujuban.

In 2011, the owner started serving kakigori in the summer when taiyaki sales would slow. The kakigori is now served all year while long lines of customers await to taste the thinly shaved ice and azuki beans. The azuki beans are boiled in a large pot for 8 hours and adds rich aroma and delicious flavor to the kakigori. The harmonious combination of sweet and sour strawberries with soft azuki beans has made "Asayake (morning sunrise)" the most popular kakigori.

Asakusa Naniwaya serves around 10 to 15 types of kakigori. Many fans revisit to taste the seasonal flavors such as sakura and pumpkin. The traditional long-loved taste of the original shop is still reflected in the kakigori here. A must-visit shop if you're visiting Asakusa.

「あさやけ」 いちご蜜・あずき・ミルク
"Asayake" - strawberry syrup, azuki beans, milk

「宇治白あん金時」 白あん・あずき・宇治蜜
"Uji shiro-an kintoki" - shiro-an (white bean paste), azuki beans, uji-matcha syrup

「コーヒーみるくといろんなものがはいったあんこ」
ココア・コーヒーミルクシロップ・アーモンド・カシューナッツ・くるみ・クコの実・こしあん(白)
"Coffee milk, anko and various things"
cocoa, coffee milk syrup, almond, cashew nuts, walnuts, wolfberry, white koshi-an (smooth white bean paste)

「みるくといろんなフルーツ」 ミルク・スイカ・りんご・キウイなど季節の果物
"Milk and various fruits" - milk, watermelon, apple, kiwi fruit and other seasonal fruits

「おいも」 安納いも・ミルク・白ごま・黒ごま・粉糖
"Sweet potato" - sweet potato, milk, white sesame seeds, black sesame seeds, sugar

浅草浪花家

「たいやき」
"Taiyaki" - fished-shaped cake filled with red bean paste

店舗情報
住所：東京都台東区浅草2-12-4
TEL：03-3842-0988

Store information
Address:2-12-4 Asakusa, Taito-ku, Tokyo
TEL:+81-3-3842-0988

たい焼き屋のかき氷2
たい焼き なみへい

　2010年1月1日に開店した「たい焼き なみへい」は、鋳型で焼く昔ながらのたい焼きのスタイルを守る長谷で人気のたい焼き屋だ。壁掛けの柱時計と小上がりにあるちゃぶ台が、懐かしい昭和の空気感を醸し出している。
　店主・濱田紳吾さんが目指しているのは、なみへいを「みんなの駄菓子屋」にしたいという夢。鹿児島から上京した店主は、大学を卒業した後にいくつかの職を経験して20代半ばでこの店を開店。美味しいものを提供したいというのはもちろんだが、昔懐かしい駄菓子屋のように、子供も大人もみんなでワイワイと楽しく過ごせる、町の人に愛される店になることがいちばんの目標だと話す。

　かき氷の提供を始めたのは、開店した年の夏のこと。
　「かき氷をやろう」と思った時に、子供の時に故郷の鹿児島で食べた鹿児島の名物「しろくま」のことを思い出した。練乳がたっぷりかかり、フルーツでしろくまの顔を表現したかき氷。大きくて美味しくて嬉しかったなぁ…と子供の頃に感じたワクワクした気持ちが心に蘇ったという。
　「せっかく作るのであれば、最高に美味しい「しろくま」を作りたい！」と試作を繰り返し、無農薬のオレンジピールをミルク練乳に加えたオリジナルのシロップを考案。かき氷の上に飾るフルーツはその時の仕入れ次第なので、フルーツが変わるとその度に表情が異なるのも楽しい。
　子供の頃大好きだった駄菓子屋で、大好きなしろくまを一個まるごと食べるという嬉しさ。この嬉しさや楽しさを、今度は自分が子供たちに与えてあげられたら、という願いを込めて濱田さんはしろくまを削る。

Kakigori from Taiyaki shops 2
Taiyaki Namihei

Opened in 2010, "Taiyaki Namihei" is a popular taiyaki shop selling taiyaki made with traditional baking molds. The wall clock and the small low table on the tatami seating area create a nostalgic atmosphere. The owner, Mr. Hamada dreams of making Namihei into an "old-fashioned candy store for everyone". Mr. Hamada is originally from Kagoshima. He built his career after graduating from university and opened this shop in his mid-twenties.

His goal is to is to make a fun shop loved by everyone in town, from children to adults, just like the candy shop from his childhood while serving delicious food.

The shop started serving kakigori from the summer of 2010.
When the owner first decided to make kakigori, he remembered the "shirokuma (polar bear)" kakigori from Kagoshima. The kakigori with plenty of condensed milk has a face of a bear decorated on top with fruits. "It was big and delicious, and I was so happy when eating it" the owner reminisced his childhood memories.

He thought, "if I was going to make kakigori, I am going to make the best shirokuma kakigori!" Through many trial and errors, the original syrup with organic orange peel and condensed milk was created. It is also fun observing the changing expression of the bear as different seasonal fruits are used according to the season.

Mr. Hamada wants to provide the same happiness and enjoyment he felt when he was a child by serving his own shirokuma to the children,

「なみへいのしろくま！」 練乳・砂糖・ヨーグルト・無農薬オレンジピール・季節の果物
"Namihei no Shirokuma!" - condensed milk, sugar, yogurt, organic orange peel, seasonal fruits

「チョコくまくん氷」 チョコシロップ・砂糖・クッキー＆フレーク・マシュマロ・ラズベリー
"Choco kuma-kun ice" - chocolate syrup, sugar, cookies, corn flakes, marshmallows, raspberries

「あんず」 信州ハーコット(あんず)・すもも・砂糖
"Apricot" - Shinshu Harcot (apricot), plum, sugar

「ナチュラルブルーハワイ」 クチナシ色素シロップ・ラムネ
"Natural Blue Hawaii" - gardenia pigment syrup, ramune (Japanese soda)

「アポロン」 とちおとめ（いちご）・チョコソース・砂糖
"Apollon" - Tochiotome strawberries, chocolate sauce, sugar

「手作りパンとたい焼き」
"Handmade bread and taiyaki"

たい焼き なみへい

店舗情報
住所：神奈川県鎌倉市長谷1-8-10
TEL：0467-24-7900
かき氷提供期間：通年
かき氷提供時間：10:00~18:00
定休日：月曜・火曜（火曜は不定休）夏期臨時休業あり
価格帯：550円～950円

Store information
Address:1-8-10 Hase, Kamakura-shi, Kanagawa
TEL:+81-467-24-7900
Kakigori serving period:all year
Kakigori serving time:10:00 – 18:00
Closed:Mondays and Tuesdays (open some Tuesdays and closed other irregular holidays)
Price range:550 - 950 yen

究極の羽氷を求めて
三日月氷菓店

2010年に開店した「三日月氷菓店」は、天然氷を使ったかき氷を通年提供する専門店だ。

当時、かき氷だけを提供する専門店は、日本全国でも数えるほどしかなく、かき氷好きの間では「柏の三日月のかき氷がすごいらしい」という噂があっという間に広まった。三日月氷菓店のかき氷は、ふわりふわりとまるで羽のような薄い氷が重なったとても繊細な氷菓子だ。息がかかっただけですうっと溶けてしまう氷の羽に、旬のフルーツを使ったシロップを染み込ませていて、その口溶けは他店ではあまり感じることができない軽さなのだ。

店主の池田さんはかき氷店をやろうと決心したとき、全国の有名なかき氷店を食べ歩いた経験があるという。氷は開店当時から日光の三ッ星氷室の天然氷を使用。毎年天然氷の切り出しの際には店を休んで参加する。物静かで口数の少ない店主だが、一つ一つの行動に職人のような一筋の強さを感じる時がある。究極の氷を削るために、機械を調節し、様々な工夫を重ねて今の形を生み出しているのである。「三日月氷菓店」のかき氷は、他では食べることのできない究極の羽氷だ。

かき氷は定番の「宇治抹茶」や「黒みつ」のほか、「生いちご」「生すいか」「生白桃」など名前の前に「生」という文字がついた限定の果実氷がある。月に一度程度限定のメニューが入れ替わり、旬の味を楽しもうと毎月通ってくるファンも多い。全てのメニューに自家製の練乳と無添加のミルクアイスがついているのもうれしい。

The ultimate feather-like ice
Mikazuki Hyokaten

A shop that specializes in kakigori called "Mikazuki Hyokaten" opened in 2010. Kakigori made from natural ice is served throughout the year.

At the time, kakigori specialty shops were rare and rumors about the delicious kakigori at Mikazuki Hyokaten quickly spread amongst kakigori-lovers. The delicate ice dessert is made from thin feather-like ice that lay on top of each other with seasonal fruit syrup poured on top.

The owner, Mr. Ikeda, went on a kakigori tasting tour around Japan before opening his own shop. The natural ice used is from Mitsuboshi Himuro (ice house) in Nikko City. Every year, the owner himself takes a day off to participate in ice harvesting. Various efforts are made in creating the ultimate feather-like ice, including regular maintenance of the ice-shaving machine. Mr. Ikeda is a quiet man, but you can feel his strengths through his artisanal behaviors. You will not be able to experience this ultimate feather-like ice anywhere else.

Apart from the classic flavors such as "Uji-matcha" (green tea from Uji) and "Kuromitsu" (brown sugar syrup), seasonal fruit flavors such as "fresh strawberries", "fresh watermelon" and "fresh white peaches" can be enjoyed. All flavors are served with homemade condensed milk and additive-free ice cream on the side. The menu is revised every month and many fans return to the shop to indulge in the limited-time seasonal flavors.

「生いちご」 いちご・砂糖・アイス・練乳
"Fresh strawberries" - strawberries, sugar, ice cream, condensed milk

「生レモン」いちご・レモン・砂糖・アイス・練乳
"Fresh lemon" - strawberries, lemon, sugar, ice cream, condensed milk

「宇治抹茶」抹茶・砂糖・アイス・練乳
"Uji-matcha" - matcha, sugar, ice cream, condensed milk

「きゃらめる」 砂糖・生クリーム・アイス・練乳
"Caramel" - sugar, fresh cream, ice cream, condensed milk

三日月氷菓店

店舗情報
住所：千葉県柏市柏1-5-5 谷澤ビル2F
TEL：04-7162-3404
かき氷提供期間：通年
かき氷提供時間：11:00~17:30LO
定休日：火曜（10月～5月は火曜・水曜）
価格帯：700円～1000円

Store information
Address:2F Tanizawa Building, 1-5-5 Kashiwa, Kashiwa-shi, Chiba
TEL:+81-4-7162-3404
Kakigori serving period:all year
Kakigori serving time:11:00 - last order at 17:30
Closed:Tuesdays (Tuesdays and Wednesdays during October to May)
Price range:700 - 1000 yen

パティシエの作るドルチェ氷
セバスチャン

　2012年に渋谷で開店したセバスチャンは、パティシエの経験を持つ店主が作るかき氷が「まるでケーキのように美しい」と評判の人気店だ。

　店主がドルチェ氷と名前をつけたかき氷は、オレンジにチョコレート、ピスタチオにフランボワーズなど、濃厚なソースやシロップを組み合わせた大人のためのかき氷。
　ホールケーキのように見えるが中は氷でできている「氷のショートケーキ」や、氷をメレンゲで覆ってきび砂糖をかけ、バーナーで炙ったクレームブリュレ風のかき氷も開発。様々なチャレンジを繰り返し、今までにない見た目と味わいのかき氷を送り出してきた。

　氷を削るのは、他のかき氷店同様にかき氷専用の氷削機だが、氷を形作る手法は他の氷店とはちょっと異なる。ケーキ型を使用して土台を作って大理石の回転台にのせ、パレットナイフや絞り出し袋に入れたソースやクリームを次々と持ち替えて、まるでケーキが組み立てられていくようにあっという間に整えてゆく。運良くカウンター席に着くことができると、その手さばきを一部始終眺められるのだ。

　現在では、日本の各地にセバスチャンの手法を取り入れた店ができ、パティシエが手がけるかき氷が、一つのかき氷のジャンルとして認識されるようになった。一人で一台食べることのできるケーキのかき氷。ついつい見とれてしまうが、溶ける前に召し上がれ。

Ice dolce created by a pâtissier
Sebastian

"Sebastian" opened 2012 in Shibuya. The owner of this popular shop is an experienced pâtissier who makes kakigori as beautiful as a cake.

    The owner has named the desserts "ice dolce" and creates various flavors through combinations of rich sauces and syrups, such as orange and chocolate or pistachio and framboise.
    After a great deal of trial and errors, this "ice dolce", kakigori that no one has ever seen or tasted before was created. The "strawberry cake" looks like an actual sponge cake but is made from ice, and the "crème brûlée" is made by covering shaved ice with meringue, sprinkling it with cane sugar and caramelizing the top with a gas burner.

    The ice is shaved with an ice-shaving machine like a usual kakigori, but then it is shaped in a unique way. Shaved ice is put into a cake mold and placed on a rotating table where spatulas, whipped cream and sauces are used to form a cake. If you are lucky enough to be seated by the counter, you will be able to get a perfect view of the owner working his skills.

    Other shops and pâtissiers around Japan have also started using the 'Sebastian method' to make kakigori and this style has now established itself as a new genre of kakigori. Very little guilt is involved in eating a whole cake made of ice, but please make sure to eat up before it melts.

「いちごのショートケーキ」 いちご・いちごピューレ・牛乳・生クリーム・ラズベリーソース・ブルーベリー・セルフィユ
"Strawberry cake" - strawberries, strawberry purée, milk, fresh cream, raspberry sauce, blueberries, chervil

「いちごのブリュレ」 いちごピューレ・アングレーズ・卵白・きび砂糖
"Strawberry brûlée" - strawberry purée, crème anglaise, egg whites, cane sugar

セバスチャン

「いちごのショートケーキ」

店舗情報
住所：東京都渋谷区神山町7-15 ホワイトハイム大嵩102
TEL：03-5738-5740
かき氷提供期間：通年
かき氷提供時間：11:30~19:00（土・日・祝日）
　　　　　　　　13:30～19:00（平日）
定休日：金曜（夏期臨時休業あり）
価格帯：1000円～1300円

Store information
Address:White Heim Otaka 102, 7-15 Kamiyamacho,
　　　　Shibuya-ku, Tokyo
TEL:+81-3-5738-5740
Kakigori serving period:all year
Kakigori serving time:11:30 - 19:00 on weekends and
　　　　　　　　　　　national holidays
　　　　　　　　　　13:30 - 19:00 on weekdays
Closed:Fridays (irregular holidays during summer season)
Price range:1000 - 1300 yen

平成を代表するかき氷 1
和キッチンかんな

2013年に世田谷に開店した和食とかき氷の店「和キッチンかんな」は世田谷公園近くのゆったりとしたスペースを持つ和風カフェ。大きな窓から光が降り注ぐ気持ちのいい空間だ。

店舗で提供されているのは近年流行したふわふわの氷に果物シロップやホイップクリームを組み合わせるスタイル。メニューには和風のテイストを組み入れたものが多いのが特徴的だ。

きな粉練乳やみたらし・紫芋などのかき氷は、見た目が可愛いだけでなく懐かしい和菓子の味がする。

これは、もともと日本料理出身の店主や和食の職人達でメニューを開発したため、醤油・きなこ・あんこといった和の食材を自然と取り入れていたからだという。

そんな和風メニューの中でも、特に注目されたのは「みたらし牛乳」のかき氷。牛乳と練乳を合わせて煮詰めた「特製牛乳」のかき氷に、添え付けのあられ・のり・しょうゆ風味のシロップを合わせるとまるでみたらし団子のような味になる。一つのかき氷で二つの味を楽しむことができる、味の変化が楽しいかき氷だ。

Kakigori of the Heisei era 1
Wa Kitchen Kanna

Wa Kitchen Kanna opened in 2013. It is a Japanese style café located near Setagaya Park with sunlight flooding through a large window creating a peaceful atmosphere.

The shop serves fluffy kakigori topped with syrup and whipped cream. It offers various Japanese flavors, such as condensed milk and kinako (roasted soybean flour), mitarashi (sweet soy sauce) and purple sweet potato.

Japanese ingredients such as soy sauce, kinako and red bean paste is mainly featured as the menu was developed by many Japanese food experts including the owner.

A popular flavor is the "mitarashi milk" kakigori. The ice is flavored with "special milk" created by a mix of milk and condensed milk. Once topped with arare (small rice crackers), seaweed and soy sauce syrup, the combination of these ingredients create the taste of mitarashi dango (mochi glazed with sweet soy sauce). This amusing kakigori allows us to enjoy multiple flavors in a single bowl.

店舗情報
住所：東京都世田谷区下馬2-43-11　2階
TEL：03-6453-2737
かき氷提供期間：通年
かき氷提供時間：11:00~18:30LO
定休日：水曜
価格帯：800円～1000円、
　　　　ミニサイズ600円

Store information
Address:2F, 2-43-11 Shimouma, Setagaya-ku, Tokyo
TEL +81-3-6453-2737
Kakigori serving period:all year
Kakigori serving time:11:00 - last order at 18:30
Closed:Wednesdays
Price range:800 - 1000 yen (regular size),
　　　　　600 yen (mini size)

「みたらしかき氷」 牛乳・練乳・醤油蜜・あられ・のり
"Mitarashi kakigori" - milk, condensed milk, soy sauce syrup, arare (small pebbles of rice crackers), seaweed

「紫芋かき氷」 紫芋・砂糖・牛乳・練乳・にしきごま
"Purple sweet potato kakigōri" - purple sweet potato, sugar, milk, condensed milk, nishiki goma (colorful sesame seeds)

「若葉」 いちご・砂糖・牛乳・抹茶
"Wakaba" - strawberries, sugar, milk, matcha

平成を代表するかき氷 2
雪うさぎ

　日光のダイニングバーで食べた羽のように薄いかき氷に感動した店主が、自身の蕎麦屋でデザートとしてかき氷を提供するようになったのが「雪うさぎ」の前身。「雪うさぎ」には、大人も子供も、いろんな人が楽しめるように20種類を超える定番メニューがずらりと並ぶ。定番メニューの他には、期間限定の旬の果物を使ったかき氷や、行事やイベントを意識したかき氷など、数種類の裏メニューも用意されている。

　特に人気が高いのは、メロンが旬を迎える頃に数量限定で提供される「丸ごとメロン」。メロン半分をそのまま器にしてかき氷を盛りつけ、生メロン果汁をたっぷりかけた贅沢なご馳走かき氷。最初はメロン味のかき氷を楽しみ、後半は程よく冷えた甘いメロンを独り占めにすることができるご馳走かき氷だ。

　もう一つ「雪うさぎ」で開店当時から人気があるメニューが「塩キャラメルグラノーラ」だ。ミルク味のかき氷の上にホイップクリームとグラノーラをトッピング。甘いキャラメルソースと岩塩をかけたかき氷は、食べ進むごとに食感や味わいが変化してゆく。まるでパフェのような、華やかで楽しいかき氷だ。

Kakigori of the Heisei era 2
Yukiusagi

The owner of Yukiusagi start serving kakigori at his own Soba noodle restaurant after he was moved by the taste of kakigori he ate in Nikko, with ice shaved as thin as a feather.

　With over 20 types of classic kakigori on the menu, everyone can indulge in their favorite flavor. The store also makes kakigori with seasonal fruits and limited-time kakigori designed for seasonal events.
　The most popular is the melon kakigori. Limited numbers are served when the melons are in season. The melon is cut in half and used as a bowl, then topped with shaved ice covered in rich melon sauce. Start out by enjoying the melon flavored kakigori and to finish, treat yourself to a cool melon all to yourself.

　Another popular flavor on the menu is the "salt caramel granola". The milk flavored shaved ice is topped with whipped cream and granola. This fun and colorful kakigori provides a flavor transformation experience as you eat through the ice covered in sweet caramel sauce and salt.

店舗情報
住所：東京都世田谷区駒沢3-18-2 オザワビル1階
TEL：03-3410-7007
かき氷提供期間：通年
かき氷提供時間：11:30〜22:00
定休日：月曜
価格帯：650円〜1000円

Store information
Address:Ozawa Building 1F, 3-18-2 Komazawa,
　　　　Setagaya-ku, Tokyo
TEL:+81-3-3410-7007
Kakigori serving period:all year
Kakigori serving time:11:30 - 22:00
Closed:Mondays
Price range:650 - 1000 yen

「生メロン」 メロン果肉・メロン果汁・ミルク
"Fresh melon" - melon, melon juice, milk

105

「塩キャラメルグラノーラ」 ミルクシロップ・キャラメルシロップ・ホイップクリーム・グラノーラ
"Salt caramel granola" - milk syrup, caramel syrup, whipped cream, granola

「かぼちゃキャラメル」 かぼちゃペースト・牛乳・練乳・キャラメル・かぼちゃの種
"Pumpkin caramel" - pumpkin paste, milk, condensed milk, caramel, pumpkin seeds

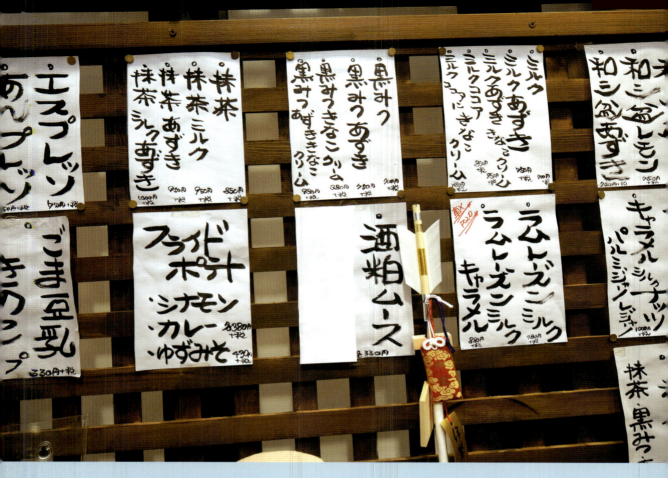

猛暑の熊谷の大人気店
慈げん

　埼玉県熊谷市は、国内の最高気温を記録したこともある「猛暑」で有名な地域である。その町に開店して19年。熊谷「慈げん」といえば、かき氷に詳しい人なら一度は耳にしたことがある人気店だ。
　もともと熊谷の小麦を使った熊谷うどんと「フライ」という薄いお好み焼きのような軽食、それから夏季限定でかき氷を提供していた「慈げん」だが、かき氷が美味しいという評判が広がり、今ではかき氷を通年提供する専門店となった。かき氷を食べるためだけに県外からこの店を目指して通う客も多い。

　その人気の理由の一つ、「慈げん」のかき氷は甘くない。いや、もちろん甘いことは甘いのだが、使っている素材を一番ひきたたせるギリギリの甘さを追求しているのだ。もともと、かき氷は暑さをしのぎ、喉の渇きを抑える食べ物である。甘すぎて、喉が乾いてしまうというようでは本末転倒なのである。
　桜のかき氷は桜の香りを、いちごのかき氷はいちごの酸味を、ミルクの美味しさや小豆の風味を楽しめる糖度を「慈げん」は知っているのである。

　「慈げん」のかき氷は冬食べても夏と同様に美味しい。実は「慈げん」では、徹底的に温度を管理して、室内の温度と湿度を、かき氷を美味しく食べられるように調整しているのである。かき氷を一番美味しいと思える状態に保つこと、これは通年かき氷を提供する上で最も大切なことかもしれない。
　「やると決めたら徹底的にやる。」
　ちょっと頑固な店主が作り上げたこだわりの強いかき氷たちが、今日もずらりと並んでいるはずだ。

Kakigori from the hottest city
Jigen

Kumagaya City is known as the "hottest city in Japan". It has been 19 years since Jigen opened in this city and it has become a popular shop that any kakigori-lover would recognize.

    Jigen originally started out serving light meals such as udon noodles made from locally grown wheat and pancake-like snacks called "fry". Kakigori was only served during the summer but the delicious dessert became so popular that it is now a specialty shop serving kakigori all year. Many people travel from afar to taste their delectable kakigori.

    Jigen is famous for its non-sweet kakigori. Of course, it is somewhat sweet, but the sweetness has been retained to a certain limit to bring out the natural flavor of the ingredients. Kakigori was originally created to quench thirst in the sweltering summer heat. It is no use if the sweetness causes further thirst.

    Jigen knows the perfect sweetness most appropriate for each ingredient. It brings out the scent in sakura, the sourness in strawberries, the deliciousness in milk and the flavor of azuki beans.

    The temperature and humidity of the shop is managed so we can indulge in kakigori anytime, even during the winter. Providing the perfect environment for eating kakigori may be the most important job for a specialty shop.

    "Once I decide, I will follow through until the end."

    Kakigori made by the strong motivation of the slightly stubborn owner will continue to be served today.

「さくら」 桜の花の塩漬け・桜の葉の塩漬け・氷砂糖
"Sakura" - salt pickled cherry blossom flowers, salt pickled cherry blossom leaves, rock sugar

「プレミアムミルクに生いちご」 いちご・砂糖・生クリーム・生乳・練乳
"Premium milk and fresh strawberries" - strawberries, sugar, fresh cream, milk, condensed milk

「プレミアムミルクにレモン with キャラメル」 レモン果汁・レモンピール・砂糖・生クリーム・生乳・自家製キャラメル
"Premium milk and lemon with caramel" - lemon juice, lemon peel, sugar, fresh cream, milk, homemade caramel

「あんプレッソ」 あずき・エスプレッソ・和三盆
"An-presso" - azuki beans, espresso, wasanbon (fine-grained Japanese sugar)

慈げん

店舗情報
住所：埼玉県熊谷市宮町2-95　間庭ビル1階
TEL：048-526-1719
かき氷提供期間：通年
かき氷提供時間：10:00~16:00
　　　　　　　（整理券配布開始時間 9:00）
定休日：不定休（Twitterで告知）
価格帯：700円～1300円

Store information
Address:Maniwa Building 1F, 2-95 Miyacho, Kumagaya-shi, Saitama
TEL:+81-48-526-1719
Kakigcri serving period:all year
Kakigcri serving time:10:00 - 16:00
　　　　　　　　　(numbered tickets handed out from 9:00)
Closed:irregular holidays (TBA on Twitter)
Price range:700 - 1300 yen

苺を楽しむかき氷
クラフトカフェ

　「むさしのくらふと陶芸スクール」が運営する「ものつくり」が体験できるカフェでは、豆にこだわったオリジナルブレンドのコーヒーと、埼玉の美味しいものを盛り込んだかき氷が美味しいと評判。
　自慢の珈琲のかき氷をはじめ、梅・桃・杏・ぶどう・柚子など季節の果物を使ったかき氷や、ハロウィン・クリスマス・お正月といった季節イベントのメニューなど、豊富なバリエーションが揃っている。
　豊富なメニューの中で最も人気があるのは、地元のいちご農園「美園いちごランド」で採れる新鮮な苺をふんだんに使った苺のかき氷だ。生いちごが旬を迎える時期には、いちご農園のオリジナル品種「レイベリー」をたっぷり贅沢にトッピング。これは「美園いちごランド」が扱う4種の苺の中で最も甘く人気のある品種で、この時期になると多くの苺ファンがかき氷目当てに訪れるという。
　その他の時期には、同じ苺農園で栽培されている、程よい酸味があって果肉が赤い「紅ほっぺ」を煮込んで自家製の苺蜜にし、一年通して苺のかき氷を提供できるようにしているという。

　そんなクラフトカフェでは、苺を様々なシロップに組み合わせて新しい楽しみ方を教えてくれる。
　例えば、苺と紅茶・苺と抹茶・苺とチョコレートというふうに、苺を主役ではなく脇役にすることで、単品では気づかなかった苺の魅力がわかるのだ。紅茶のフレーバーに苺の香りが加わって両方の香りを互いに引き立てあったり、濃厚なチョコレートソースに苺が加わることによって爽やかな酸味がアクセントとなったり。甘くて、酸っぱくて、爽やかで、濃厚。クラフトカフェの苺のかき氷はいろんな面を見せてくれる。きっといつもの苺のかき氷とは一味違う、大人の苺のかき氷に出会うことができるだろう。

116

The taste of strawberries
Craft Café

At this café operated by "Musashino Craft Ceramic Arts School", you can make crafts, enjoy kakigori made with tasty local foods and sip on an original blend coffee made from carefully selected coffee beans.

    Coffee kakigori and seasonal fruit kakigori such as Japanese plum, peaches, apricots, grapes and yuzu are served at "Craft Café". You can also enjoy the limited-time original flavors during Halloween, Christmas and new years.

    The strawberry kakigori is most popular, it is made with strawberries grown in "Misono Ichigo Land", a local farm. The "Rayberry" strawberry is the sweetest and most popular type of strawberries grown at this farm and when in season, many strawberry-lovers gather to taste the kakigori topped with this strawberry.

    During other seasons of the year "Beni-Hoppe" strawberries grown in the same farm is boiled to create strawberry syrup, so we can enjoy strawberry kakigori throughout the year.

    At Craft Café, we can discover new flavors through unique combinations of strawberries and various types of syrups. Strawberries are paired with black tea, matcha or chocolate to support these main flavors. For example, strawberry added to black tea can expand the aroma of black tea or it can be used to add a dash of sour flavor boost to the rich chocolate sauce. Whether sweet, sour, refreshing or rich, you'll be able to rediscover a new side of strawberry kakigori at Craft Café.

美園いちごランドの「レイベリー」
"Rayberry" - strawberries from "Misono Ichigo Land"

「スペシャル苺」 生苺・グラニュー糖・レモン汁・練乳・ホイップクリーム
"Special strawberry" - fresh strawberries, granulated sugar, lemon juice, condensed milk, whipped cream

「ほんのり桜」 桜の花の塩漬け・桜ソース・ピスタチオ・うぐいすきな粉・生苺・白あん・イチゴシロップ・抹茶
"Honnori sakura" - salt pickled cherry blossom flowers, cherry blossom sauce, pistachio, uguisu kinako (green roasted soybean flour), fresh strawberries, shiro-an (white bean paste), strawberry syrup, matcha

「ベリーショコラ」 ショコラソース・チョコチップ入り練乳・生苺・ラズベリーソース・ココアパウダー
"Berry chocolate" - chocolate sauce, condensed milk with chocolate chip, fresh strawberries, raspberry sauce, cocoa powder

「苺キャラメルミルクティー」 生苺・グラニュー糖・アッサムティー・練乳・グラノーラ・キャラメルソース
"Strawberry caramel milk tea" - fresh strawberries, granulated sugar, Assam tea, condensed milk, granola, caramel sauce

「珈琲キャラメル」 珈琲（ペルー）・グラニュー糖・コーヒーゼリー・キャラメルソース
"Coffee caramel" - coffee (from Peru), granulated sugar, coffee jelly, caramel sauce

クラフトカフェ

店舗情報
住所：埼玉県さい
TEL：048-882-0
かき氷提供期間：
かき氷提供時間：

定休日：木曜
価格帯：500円〜

Store informati
Address:1695-1 D
 Saitama
TEL:+81-48-882-0
Kakigori serving p
Kakigori serving t

Closed:Thursdays
Price range:500 -

「宇治金時」 抹茶・砂糖・小豆
"Uji kintoki" - matcha, sugar, azuki beans

たべあるきかき氷
あずきや安堂

「あずきや安堂」は東京都調布市の北口、天神通り商店街の中にある今川焼きの専門店だ。「今川焼き」とは、小麦粉を使った生地に餡を入れて焼き上げた和菓子で「大判焼き（全国）」、「回転焼き（関西・九州地区）」、「二重焼き（中国地方）」など多くの呼び名を持つ昔ながらの日本の和菓子である。商店街や神社の門前町のほか、お祭りや屋台で売られることも多く、古くから日常的なおやつとして親しまれてきた懐かしの味である。

固定の店舗を持つ今川焼き屋では、夏になるとジュースやアイス、かき氷を提供することが多く、子供達は店先を通りかかると、冬は今川焼き・夏はかき氷を買ってもらえることを楽しみにしたものだ。「あずきや安堂」では、5月から10月まで期間限定でかき氷を提供。テイクアウト専門で安価な値段であるにもかかわらず、本格的なシロップを提供することで注目を集めてきた人気店である。

一児の母でもある店主の「安全で美味しい今川焼き」というコンセプトはかき氷でも同じ。大量にシロップを作らず、旬の果物などのシロップを少しづつ作って数量限定で提供している。
かき氷を始めた頃からある「福原農園の無農薬甘夏かき氷」は、皮の部分まで安心して食べられるので、ほろ苦く優しい酸味の甘夏ピールがたっぷり添えられている。実はこの蜜、一つ一つ皮をむいて甘夏の実を薄皮から取り出し、ピールもなんども煮て苦味を抜いたとても手のかかるもの。優しい味がするのは、やさしい気持ちで作られているからかもしれない。

Kakigori on the go
Azukiya Ando

"Azukiya Ando" specializes in imagawa-yaki and is located inside a shopping arcade in Chofu, Tokyo. Imagawa-yaki is a Japanese-style pancake filled with red bean paste. It is a traditional snack loved by many is usually sold in shopping arcades, shrines, temple towns and in small stalls at festivals. It is also called oban-yaki (nationally), kaiten-yaki (in Kansai and Kyushu) or nijyu-yaki (in Chugoku).

Many imagawa-yaki shops sell juice, ice cream or kakigori during the summer. When children pass by the shop, many anticipate a treat of imagawa-yaki in winter and kakigori in summer. Kakigori at Azukiya Ando is only served from May to October. The shop became popular for their reasonably priced take-away kakigori topped with authentic syrup.

The owner is a mother herself, and she believes in the concept of providing "safe and delicious" food. She does not produce her syrup in masses but carefully makes small amounts made from seasonal fruits.
Even though it is very time-consuming to make the syrup for organic Amanatsu orange kakigori, it has been on the menu since the shop first started serving kakigori. It is topped with plenty of organic orange peel creating a slightly bitter but gentle flavor. The owner peels and extracts the flesh of each orange by hand, then the skin is boiled several times to rid of the bitterness. The gentle flavor may be coming from the gentle kindness put into each kakigori.

「特製いちごみるく」いちご・砂糖・牛乳・練乳
"Special strawberry milk" - strawberries, sugar, milk, condensed milk

「福原農園の無農薬甘夏」甘夏・砂糖
"Organic Amanatsu orange from Fukuhara Farm" - Amanatsu orange, sugar

あずきや安堂

今川焼きは毎日焼きたてが店頭に並んでいる。
Freshly baked imagawa-yaki

店舗情報
住所：東京都調布市布田1-36-10
TEL：042-455-1221
かき氷提供期間：5月初旬〜10月末
かき氷提供時間：10:30〜19:00
定休日：不定休（年に数日）
価格帯：500円〜700円

Store information
Address:1-36-10 Fuda, Chofu-shi, Tokyo
TEL:+81-42-455-1221
Kakigori serving period:early May - end of October
Kakigori serving time:10:30 - 19:00
Closed:irregular holidays (few times per year)
Price range:500 - 700 yen

昭和を味わうかき氷
梅むら

　昭和25年、長野から上京して来た店主の若林さんは浅草の「梅むら」という和菓子屋に修行に入る。わずか14歳だった彼はその店で18年間修行を積み、やがて名前を継いで現在の場所に「梅むら」を開店させた。当時この界隈には高級料亭が多く、料亭の顧客や芸者さんから人気の高い甘味処であったという。

　「梅むら」を代表する「豆かん」は、北海道産の赤えんどう豆を柔かく炊き、天草から作った寒天と黒蜜を加えたとてもシンプルな甘味だ。あんみつを提供する際に「あんこ抜きで」「フルーツ抜きで」という注文があり、思いきって豆と寒天だけの甘味にしたという。さっぱりとした「豆かん」にとろみのある黒蜜を組み合わせるとこれが大当たり。現在でも一番人気の甘味である。

　豆は驚くほどたっぷりと器に盛られ「こんなに!?」と驚く人もいるが、この豆が抜群に美味い。「この店に来て豆が食べられるようになった」とよく言われるというのも頷ける。豆の風味を残しながら、ほっこりと柔らかく絶妙の炊き具合。この豆かんにふわふわの氷をのせたものが「梅むら」でしか出会えないかき氷、「氷豆かんてん」である。

　氷部分には味はつけないのが関東下町風のかき氷の盛りつけ方で、かまくらのように氷を掘って「豆かん」となじませながら食べる。氷が次第に黒蜜で染まり、氷の中から顔を出した寒天と豆を一緒に頬張るともう止まらない。あっという間に完食してしまう。

　また、最近あまり見なくなった、昭和の人気のかき氷「あんず氷」もこの店では健在だ。干しあんずを煮て白蜜を加え、あんずの甘酸っぱさで氷を食べる。とても繊細で、味が深く美味しいかき氷。古き良き時代を思い出させてくれるような、懐かしのかき氷を味わうことができる。

Kakigori of the Showa era
Umemura

Mr. Wakabayashi started training at a wagashi shop named "Umemura" when he was only 14. After working here for 18 years, he inherited the name and opened his own Umemura in Asakusa. It was a popular shop amongst customers and Geishas who visited the high-class restaurants around this area.

"Mame-kan" is a simple dessert made by adding softly boiled red peas to kanten (agar) and kuromitsu (brown sugar syrup). The perfect combination of flavors and textures have made it the most popular dessert on the menu for years.

The delicious beans are perfectly boiled, making it soft but maintaining its original flavor. The amount of beans may surprise some people, but even those who are not fond of beans say they've acquired a taste for it after eating mame-kan. "Kori mame-kanten" is kakigori created by topping fluffy ice on top of these beans.

There is a certain way to enjoy this kakigori as the ice itself is not flavored. First the ice is eaten with "mame-kan" through a hole, as the kuromitsu dampens and melts the ice, now the beans and kanten can be eaten together.

The "apricot kakigori" is also a long-running favorite in this shop. The sourness of boiled dried apricots with shiromitsu (white sugar syrup) add flavor to the ice. It is a beautiful kakigori delicate and rich in flavor. At Umemura, you'll be able to indulge in nostalgic kakigori that will remind you a little of the good old Japan.

器の中には名物「豆かん（豆寒天）」がぎっしり詰まっている。
The bowl is packed full of their famous dessert, "mamekan"

「氷豆かんてん」 赤えんどう豆・黒糖(沖縄)・上白糖・寒天
"Kori mame-kanten" - boiled red peas with kanten (agar) and kuromitsu (brown sugar syrup)

梅むら

「氷あんず」
"Kori Anzu"

「豆寒天」
"Mame-kanten"

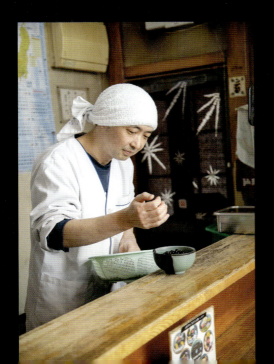

店舗情報
住所：東京都台東区浅草3-22-12
TEL：03-3873-6992
かき氷提供期間：通年
かき氷提供時間：12:30~19:00
定休日：日曜
価格帯：550円～750円

Store information
Address:3-22-12 Asakusa, Taito-ku, Tokyo
TEL:+81-3-3873-6992
Kakigori serving period:all year
Kakigori serving time:12:30 - 19:00
Closed:Sundays
Price range:550 - 750 yen

池永鉄工株式会社

　昭和25年から「SWAN印」の氷削機を製造している池永鉄工株式会社では、大阪の自社工場で部品を一つ一つ職人が加工し組み立て、昔ながらの「Made in Japan」を守り続けている。切れ味が持続する特殊ステンレス鋼の刃を使用しており、錆に強く衛生的で手入れが簡単であることが特徴だ。
　短時間で大量の氷を削り出すことのできる業務用・最上位機種のSI-100Sのほか、モーター音が静かで鋳物の雰囲気を残したSI-150SS、どんな飲食店スタイルにも馴染むようなスタイリッシュでシックなデザインを採用しているSI-150C（Cygne）など、用途に合わせて様々な種類の氷削機を提案している。

Ikenaga Iron Works Co., Ltd.

Ikenaga Iron Works is a metal casting manufacturer that has been producing "SWAN" ice-shaving machines since 1950. Each machine is assembled by a craftsman in traditional "Made in Japan" style. The blades are made of special stainless steel to maintain sharpness. It is also rust resistant making it clean and easy to maintain.
　Various types of ice-shaving machines can be selected according to their intended use. High-end professional use "SI_100" can quickly shave large amounts of ice, "SI_150SS" has an old-fashioned design with a quiet motor and "Cygne" maintains the performance of 150SS even with its stylish design that blends into any type of shop.

「SI-100S」
ブロック氷専用の業務用最上位機種。耐久性が強く、短時間で大量のかき氷を連続で削ることができるので、イ▢
店などで人気。氷を盛り付ける空間（盤下）が広く、盛り付けしやすく設計されている。
High-end professional-use model for shaving ice blocks. It is high in durability and can continuously shave lar▢
of ice in a short period of time. The space under the ice outlet is broad, making it easy to shave ice into bowls.

「Cygne　SI-150C」

アルミダイキャストを使用し軽量化を実現。スクエアなフォルムで落ち着いたデザインなので、スタイリッシュな空間にも和風の空間にも馴染みオープンキッチンに最適。静音タイプでモーター音も静か。

The lightweight machine is made by aluminum die casting. The sophisticated design fits into any environment and is suitable for open kitchens. The silent motor also provides quiet operation.

「SI_3B」

昭和時代の懐かしい手動かき氷機の雰囲気をそのまま残した大型手動式氷削機。鋳物で作られたボディは安定力抜群。機並みの切削能力を持つ。ギヤ駆動で回転効率も良く、丈夫で故障が少ない設計となっている。

A manually operated ice-shaving machine with an antique design. The stable body is made by metal casting and the ability is equivalent to that of an electric machine. The gear driven machine is highly durable.

株式会社中部コーポレーション

　野菜調理器や食材調理器といった厨房機器を広く扱う中部コーポレーションは、近年は氷削機の開発に力を注ぎ、毎年のように新機種を発表している。

　レストラン・カフェ・甘味処といった店舗向けの業務用氷削機「Hatsuyuki（初雪）」シリーズは、南日本を中心に広く愛されてきたが、2011年に新シリーズ「BASYS（ベイシス）」を発表。誰でもふわふわのかき氷が簡単に再現できるように改良され、軽量でありながら羽のような口どけの良いかき氷を削ることができる。

　全ての機種に、鎌倉時代より続く伝統と技を受け継ぐ切れ味の鋭い『美濃の刃物』を使用している。

Chubu Corporation-Network

Chubu Corporation offers various cooking and kitchen equipment. Recently, the company has been focusing on developing ice-shaving machines and new models are released almost every year.

　The "Hatsuyuki" series is a professional-use machine used mainly in restaurants, cafés and Japanese style cafés in Southern regions of Japan. The new and improved "BASYS" series was announced in 2011. It allows for anyone to make light and fluffy kakigori.

　The sharp blades used for their machines are called "Blades of Mino". The traditional technique of creating this blade has been passed down since the Kamakura era.

「BASYS LL（ベイシス ロングレー）HB600A」
ベイシスの扱いやすさとふわふわの削りはそのままに、足を長くして作業空間を広くした機種。
背の高いかき氷を作ることができ、空間が広いことで氷を削りながらの盛りつけも自由にできる。
This model has the same features as the easy-to-operate "BASYS" that can produce fluffy ice but with lor
room can be used for making tall and beautiful kakigori.

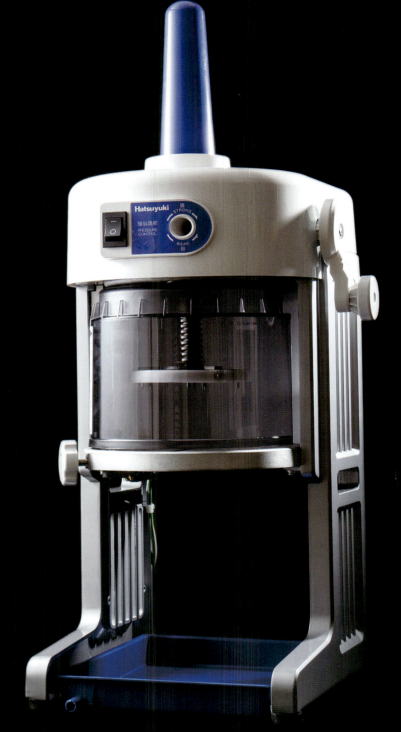

「BASYS(ベイシス)HB310B」
初心者でも操作しやすく、本格的な氷削機の中では16キロと軽量で持ち運びしやすい。
ふわふわとした削りが簡単に再現できると、初心者・専門家ともに人気が高い機種。
Portable and easy-to-operate machine only weighing 16kg. It allows for anyone to make fluffy shaved ice, making it popular for beginners and specialists.

「HA110S」
昔と変わらない懐かしいスタイルの手動氷削機。電源がとれない場所や期間限定で提供するカフェなどに人気。軽量で持ち運びしやすいが、業務用の貫目氷（13センチ角）を削ることができる。
Old-fashioned manual ice-shaving machine. It is popular for use in places without power outlets or in shops that sell kakigori for limited periods only. It is lightweight and portable, but strong enough to shave large blocks of ice.

明治時代の業務用氷削機

　大工道具の鉋（かんな）を逆さにして足をつけたようなこの機械は、明治時代に使われていた業務用の氷削機。
　氷をこの上で滑らせて薄く削っていた。現在でも同型の氷削り機を使ってかき氷を提供している店がある。

Ice-shaving machines in the Meiji era

This tool may look like a plane for shaving wood, but it is a professional-use ice-shaving tool from the Meiji era.

　The ice was thinly shaved by sliding it along this apparatus. Some shops still make their kakigori using this tool.

家庭用氷削機の歴史

　日本の家庭用氷削機の歴史は、冷蔵庫の普及に伴って幕を開けた。日本に家庭用の第一号電気冷蔵庫が現れたのは昭和初期。最初は冷凍機能は備わっていなかったが、やがて冷凍機能が加わり、昭和40年代には広く電気冷凍冷蔵庫が普及した。こうして家で氷が作られるようになり、家で作った氷でかき氷を作る家庭用氷削機が各社から製造されるようになったのだ。
　この時代のかき氷機は、どうしたらうまくかき氷を削れるか工夫を凝らし、その形態も様々であった。
　氷をセッティングする位置も、縦型あり横型あり。彩りも非常に鮮やかで眺めているとワクワクしてくる。
　昭和50年代には、ハンドルを回すと目がきょろきょろと動く「きょろちゃん」が大人気となって、手回し型の家庭用氷削機が広く浸透した。最も家庭用の氷削機が華やかだった時代である。
　この後は電気を使う電動式が増え、手回しの氷削機は少しづつ需要が少なくなっていくこととなった。

History of household ice-shaving machines

The history of household ice-shaving machines started in Japan with the arrival of refrigerators. In the 1930s refrigerators did not have freezing functions but by the late 60s refrigerator-freezers became common. Companies started producing household ice-shaving machines as ice became easier to make.

　Companies produced different forms of machines to make the best homemade kakigori. Ice could be set horizontally or vertically, and many color variations were available. In the 70s "Kyoro-chan", a bear-shaped ice-shaving machine became a hit in Japan. The eyes on this cute bear move as the handle is rotated.

　Recently, electric machines are more popular with declining demand for manual ice-shaving machines.

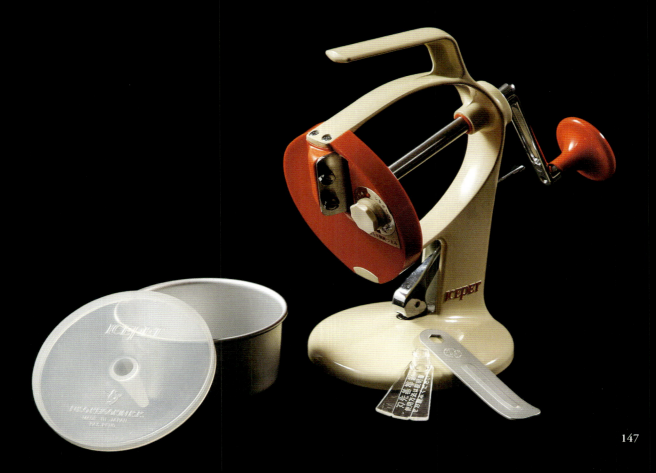

協栄物産株式会社 「サマーペット」
専用氷のカップで氷を作って削る。色使いがとても可愛い。

Kyoei Bussan Co.,Ltd. "Summer Pet"
Cute colored machine used for shaving ice made in a special cup.

扶桑軽合金株式会社 「アイスペット」
氷の薄さを調節できるうえ、テーブルに固定できる仕掛けもついている。

Fuso Keigokin K.K "Ice Pet"
The thinness of ice can be adjusted, and the machine is able to be fixed onto the table.

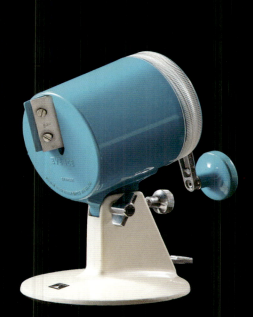

ナショナル魔法瓶工業株式会社 「エベアアイス」
専用氷を作らなくても製氷機で作った氷を削ることができる。

National Vacuum Bottle Co., Ltd. "Evia Ice"
Special ice is not need for this machine. It can shave ice made in usual ice trays from home.

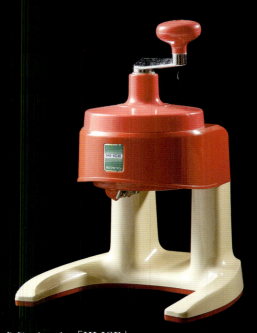

象印マホービン 「HI ICE」
昭和43年発売　包丁で有名なヘンケルの刃を使用した本格派。

ZOJIRUSHI CORPORATION "HI ICE"
Released in 1968. A full-fledged machine with Henckels blades famous for knives.

タイガー魔法瓶工業株式会社 「きょろちゃん」 2016年に再発売したが2018年をもって販売を終了。
Tiger Corporation. "Kyoro-chan" Reintroduced in 2016 but sales have ended in 2018.

あとがき

　日本人なら一度は食べたことがある氷菓子「かき氷」。

　夏休みの海の家や花火大会の屋台で売られる「レインボー」、和菓子屋で提供される「宇治金時」をはじめ、暑い日本の夏にはあちらこちらで「氷」の旗が吊るされている。

　大人になってからあまり食べる機会がなかったのだが、あるとき氷卸屋で食べたかき氷に驚愕した。

　味のない氷を削り、甘い蜜をかけて食べるというとてもシンプルな食べ物なのに、シンプルな故に奥深く、削る人の腕で大きく味わいが変化することに驚いた。

　それから「あそこのかき氷が美味しいらしい」「あの削り手（かき氷を削る人）はすごい技術だ」と食べ歩き仲間と話しながら食べ歩くうちに、機械に興味が湧き、氷自体に興味がでて、気がつくと一年中かき氷を追いかける生活を送るようになっていた。

　かき氷の主役は氷である。口どけの良いかき氷は見た目も美しく、美しいかき氷はたいていの場合その味わいも素晴らしい。そんな美しいかき氷をこの本を通して多くの人に知ってもらい、いつか口にしていただければ嬉しいと思う。

　最後に、この本を作るチャンスをくださった旭屋出版さん。氷の美しさを引き出してくださったカメラマンの宮本さん、岩崎さん。根気よく付き合っていただいたデザイナーの上筋さん。かき氷を作っていただいた店舗の皆さん。そのほかの関係者各位に、深く感謝申し上げます。

Epilogue

"Kakigori" is a dessert that any Japanese person would have tasted at least once. During the Japanese summer, many signs for kakigori pop up at various locations. The classic "rainbow" kakigori sold at beach houses and stalls, or the traditional "Uji-kintoki" kakigori sold at a wagashi shop to name a few.

I didn't have many opportunities to eat kakigori after becoming an adult, but one day I was struck by the deliciousness of a kakigori I ate at an ice shop.

The simple but profound dessert is made by shaving taste-less ice and is eaten with sweet syrup. I was surprised by the differing taste of kakigori at each shop, depending on the skills of the person shaving the ice.

After that, I collected and shared information with my friends saying, "the kakigori at that shop is great!" and "the ice-shaving technique by that master is amazing!" becoming interested in the ice itself and even the ice-shaving machines. When I realized, I was immersed in the world of kakigori, searching for kakigori all year.

The star of the kakigori is of course the ice. Smooth melting ice is visually beautiful, and beautiful ice is generally delicious. I would be more than happy if people discover the beauty of kakigori through this book.

Lastly, I would like to express my gratitude to Asahiya Publishing for giving us the opportunity to publish this book, Mr. Miyamoto and Mr. Iwasaki for taking beautiful pictures, the designer, Mr. Uesuji for your perseverance, all the shops featured for making the kakigori, and to everyone else involved in the making of this book.

協力

池永鉄工株式会社
株式会社中部コーポレーション
一般社団法人日本かき氷協会

日本の美しいかき氷

発行日　　2019年6月3日　　初版発行
　　　　　2019年7月26日　　第2版発行

著　者　　一般社団法人日本かき氷協会代表　小池 隆介
　　　　　市場 ゆりこ
発行者　　早嶋 茂
制作者　　永瀬 正人
発行所　　株式会社旭屋出版
　　　　　東京都新宿区愛住町23番地2　ベルックス新宿ビルⅡ　6階　〒160-0005
　　　　　電話03-5369-6423（販売）
　　　　　03-5369-6424（編集）
　　　　　FAX 03-5369-6431（販売）
　　　　　URL http:www//asahiya-jp.com/

印刷・製本　株式会社シナノパブリッシングプレス

編　集　　小池 隆介
デザイン　アップライン株式会社　上筋 英彌
撮　影　　宮本雅通写真事務所　宮本 雅通
　　　　　岩崎 包明
英文作成　古藤 あや
校　正　　辻 真優子

郵便振替　00150-1-19572
ISBN978-4-7511-1385-1　C2077

定価はカバーに表示してあります。乱丁・落丁本はお取替え致します
本書の記事・写真などを無断で複写（コピー）・転写、Webで記載することを禁じます
ⒸRyusuke Koike ＆Yuriko Ichiba,2019 Printed in Japan